ARMOURED DINOSAURS

BY **'DINO' DON LESSEM**

ILLUSTRATIONS BY **JOHN BINDON**

LERNER BOOKS · LONDON · NEW YORK · MINNEAPOLIS

To Ken Carpenter, armoured dinosaur expert

Text copyright © 2005 by Dino Don, Inc.
Illustrations copyright © 2005 by John Bindon

This book was first published in the Unites States of America as Armored Dinosaurs in 2005.
First published in the United Kingdom in 2008 by
Lerner Books,
Dalton House,
60 Windsor Avenue,
London SW19 2RR

This edition was updated and edited for UK publication by Discovery Books Ltd.,
Unit 3, 37 Watling Street, Leintwardine, Shropshire SY7 0LW.

Words in **bold type** are explained in the glossary on page 32.

British Library Cataloguing in Publication Data

Lessem, Don
  Armoured dinosaurs. - (Meet the dinosaurs)
  1. Ornithischia - Juvenile literature
  I. Title
  567.9'15

  ISBN-13: 978 1 58013 337 1

Photographs courtesy of: © Charles Gilmore, Smithsonian Institute, National Museum of Natural History,
p. 28; American Museum of Natural History, p. 29; © Dinamation International Corporation, p. 30; © Pat
Crowe, p. 31.

Printed in China

TABLE OF CONTENTS

MEET THE ARMOURED DINOSAURS

WELCOME, DINOSAUR FANS!

I'm 'Dino' Don. Dinosaurs are my favourite animals. The armoured dinosaurs had strong armour for protection. Here are some fast facts on the armoured dinosaurs you'll meet in this book. Have fun!

ANKYLOSAURUS
Length: 7.5 metres
Home: western North America
Time: 65 million years ago

EDMONTONIA
Length: 7 metres
Home: western North America
Time: 75 million years ago

EUOPLOCEPHALUS
Length: 5 metres
Home: western North America
Time: 75 million years ago

GASTONIA
Length: 6 metres
Home: western North America
Time: 130 million years ago

HUAYANGOSAURUS
Length: 4 metres
Home: eastern Asia
Time: 170 million years ago

MINMI
Length: 3 metres
Home: Australia
Time: 110 million years ago

PINACOSAURUS
Length: 5.5 metres
Home: eastern Asia
Time: 80 million years ago

STEGOSAURUS
Length: 7.5 metres
Home: western North America
Time: 145 million years ago

SAVED BY ARMOUR

Here comes a hungry *Albertosaurus!* It's much bigger and faster than *Edmontonia*. But *Edmontonia* is covered with bony plates and spikes. *Albertosaurus* cannot bite or scratch through this thick **armour**.

THE TIME OF THE ARMOURED DINOSAURS

Huayangosaurus

Stegosaurus

170 million
years ago

145 million
years ago

Edmontonia, Albertosaurus and other dinosaurs lived on land millions of years ago. Dinosaurs were like reptiles in some ways. They laid eggs, as snakes and other reptiles do. But dinosaurs weren't reptiles. Birds are closer relatives of dinosaurs than reptiles are.

Minmi — 110 million years ago

Pinacosaurus — 80 million years ago

Ankylosaurus — 65 million years ago

One group of dinosaurs had armoured bodies. Scientists think that armour helped protect these dinosaurs from **predators**. Predators are animals that kill and eat other animals. The armoured dinosaurs weren't predators. They ate only plants.

DINOSAUR FOSSIL FINDS

The numbers on the map on page 11 show some of the places where people have found fossils of the dinosaurs in this book. You can match each number on the map to the name and picture of the dinosaurs on this page.

1. Ankylosaurus

2. Edmontonia

3. Euoplocephalus

4. Gastonia

5. Huayangosaurus

6. Minmi

7. Pinacosaurus

8. Stegosaurus

We know about armoured dinosaurs from the traces they left behind, called **fossils**. Bony plates, spikes and footprints help scientists understand how armoured dinosaurs were built. But fossils can't tell us what colour a dinosaur was. They can't tell us how its skin and muscles looked.

Still, fossils are our best clues to the puzzle of how armoured dinosaurs might have lived. People have found fossils of these strange animals all over the world.

PLATES, SPIKES AND CLUBS

The deadly predator *Utahraptor* is attacking.
It slashes at *Gastonia* with sharp claws that
are as long as a carving knife. But *Gastonia*
has the heaviest armour of any dinosaur.
Utahraptor cannot slice through it. In time,
the tired predator gives up.

Meat-eating dinosaurs were faster and smarter than armoured dinosaurs. But spikes and thick plates kept armoured dinosaurs safe from attack. Even their eyelids were covered with bone!

The giant back plates of *Stegosaurus* may
have scared off some predators. But the
plates were probably built more for show
than for protection. This big male shows off
his plates to attract a female.

Back plates may have also helped heat and cool *Stegosaurus*. The plates may have soaked up the sun's heat when *Stegosaurus* was cold. And they may have given off heat when it was hot. Heating and cooling probably wasn't easy for an animal the size of a small lorry!

Euoplocephalus swishes its big, armoured tail club. Any animal would be careful around such a powerful weapon. These *Pachycephalosaurus* are peaceful plant eaters. Why is the armoured dinosaur aiming its club at them?

The dome-headed dinosaurs want to munch on the same plants that *Euoplocephalus* is eating. Armoured dinosaurs could reach only plants that grew near the ground, like shrubs and ferns. A low, fast-moving tail club may have helped some armoured dinosaurs protect their meals.

Can back spikes and body armour save
Ankylosaurus from *Tyrannosaurus rex*?
Maybe. But *Ankylosaurus* has no armour on
its belly. The *T rex* tries to flip *Ankylosaurus*
to reach this soft flesh.

Ankylosaurus squats down low on its powerful legs. This armoured giant weighs as much as four cars. It is so heavy and so close to the ground that *T rex* cannot flip it over. Squatting probably helped many armoured dinosaurs survive attack.

LIFE AND DEATH

How were armoured dinosaurs born?
Scientists think they hatched from eggs,
the way other dinosaurs did. Armoured
dinosaurs were very small when they
hatched.

We don't know if newborns like this *Minmi* had armour. If not, predators probably found them easy to kill. Armoured mothers may have nested in groups. That way, they could protect the eggs and newborns.

A young *Huayangosaurus* has just hatched.
It wanders from its nest. Nearby, two hungry
Gasosaurus wait to snap it up. The newborn's
parents and other adults arrive just in time.
Together they scare off the *Gasosaurus*.

Huayangosaurus had no tail club to defend itself. Its back plates were not very big. But a group of these dinosaurs might still have been able to scare away large predators.

Armour could not always keep dinosaurs
safe. These young *Pinacosaurus* huddle
together beneath a sand dune. They are
trapped in a fierce sandstorm.

Armoured dinosaurs faced many dangers besides hungry meat eaters. Floods and storms ended the lives of many. But armoured dinosaurs lived successfully all over the world for 100 million years.

ARMOURED DINOSAUR MYSTERIES

The last armoured dinosaurs died out suddenly 65 million years ago. So did the rest of the dinosaurs. What happened? Scientists are still trying to solve this mystery. Many think that an object from space called an **asteroid** smashed into the Earth.

The asteroid's crash with the Earth may have started fires and made volcanoes explode. Dust may have filled the air and blocked out sunlight. These changes would have killed dinosaurs, other animals and many plants.

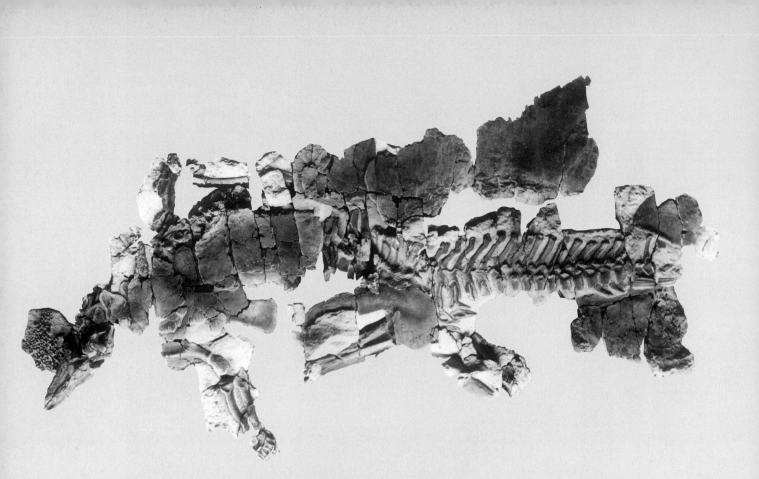

The story of *Stegosaurus* is another famous
armoured dinosaur mystery. People first
found *Stegosaurus* fossils more than 100
years ago. Some bones were missing from
the skeleton. The back plates lay flat on the
ground. They were not joined to the
skeleton's back.

Scientists could not tell how the plates used to fit on the body of a living *Stegosaurus*. Did it have one row of plates or two? For years, scientists built models of *Stegosaurus* in different ways. Artists drew it in different ways too.

Scientists in Colorado found new clues to the *Stegosaurus* mystery during the 1990s. They dug up skeletons of *Stegosaurus* with almost every bone still in place. These fossils showed that *Stegosaurus* did have two rows of plates on its back.

The *Stegosaurus* mystery has been solved. But people will always want to learn more about armoured dinosaurs such as *Stegosaurus* and this *Gastonia*. They are among the strangest, most interesting animals that have lived on the Earth.

GLOSSARY

armour: bony plates and spikes on the bodies of some dinosaurs

asteroid: a large rocky lump that moves in space

fossils: the remains, tracks or traces of something that lived long ago

predators: animals that hunt and eat other animals

INDEX